SMP 11-16

Using investigations

An introduction to ways of working

CAMBRIDGE
UNIVERSITY PRESS

Published by the Press Syndicate of the University of Cambridge
The Pitt Building, Trumpington Street, Cambridge CB2 1RP
40 West 20th Street, New York, NY 10011–4211, USA
10 Stamford Road, Oakleigh, Melbourne 3166, Australia

First published 1989
Second printing 1993

Printed in Great Britain at the University Press, Cambridge

ISBN 0 521 37884 2

Typeset by DMD, St Clements, Oxford

Contents

Preface

The aim of this book is to provide an introduction to the use of investigations in the classroom. Many teachers are wary of being placed in situations where they feel insecure because they cannot see where the activity may lead. The presentation of the investigations is an attempt to provide a possible path through the activity which will give inexperienced teachers a measure of confidence. More experienced teachers may find some of the ideas useful. We hope the book will be used in as flexible a way as possible.

The following people contributed to the writing of the book.

Graham Ambridge	Michael Darby
Colin Banwell	Tony Gardiner
Tony Burghall	Bob Hartman
Colin Clark	Sandra Scott
Peter Critchley	Diana Sharvill

In addition thanks go to teachers in the schools that trialled the draft versions of the tasks.

Introduction

Background

Since 1982, with the publication of the Cockcroft Report, the HMI discussion Document: Mathematics 5–16 and the advent of the GCSE, there has been much talk of mathematical investigations in the classroom.

Mathematical *content* had previously been the sole focus of most mathematics teachers. More recently, the *processes* of teaching and learning have taken on far more significance.

Mathematics cannot be adequately defined solely in terms of content. If we believe that processes are important, we need to consider how best we can develop the relevant behaviour in our pupils. Investigations have much to contribute. There is no doubt that learning by exploring situations is a powerful way to involve children with the mathematics of other people and the mathematics within themselves.

However, investigations are only a means to an end. The ultimate objective is to inject something of the investigative spirit into our teaching. Investigations should therefore not be seen as another piece of content to be done merely on a wet Friday afternoon or because it happens to be the title of the next chapter in the course book you are using.

Many teachers will feel the need for experience of investigations before they are ready to adopt an investigative approach in their teaching. Others may feel that they already have sufficient experience, confidence and the skills to move in this direction.

What we are trying to put in

Perhaps the four most important ingredients in an investigative approach are:

- It should be pupil centred.
- It should involve using processes that will lead to the understanding of concepts, rules or relationships.
- It should generate mathematical activity.
- It should generate mathematical discussion.

The starting point should be simple; for example, a problem on which all pupils can make some genuine progress. Apparatus should be available in case some pupils require 'concrete' support, though it is not always wise to hand it out at the outset. Its use can greatly benefit understanding, and may speed up the acquisition of the results or even the solution. Opportunities should be provided for the sharing of ideas and experiences and for the interaction between teacher and pupil(s) and between pupil(s) and pupil(s).

Getting started

How you introduce an investigation, whether it be to a group or to a class, is of crucial importance. You need to attract their attention and generate enthusiasm. However, the starting point and the lesson structure needs to take into consideration:

- the experience of the group
- the ability of the group
- methods of working (group, class, individual)
- content or processes you wish to develop
- the problem you wish to solve
- whether the further development should be on a group, class or individual basis.

Investigating should become an integral part of mathematics teaching. Pupils may find this approach is not in keeping with their ideas of what teaching (and learning) is all about. Therefore, they may have to change their ways. It is worth being patient; little by little they will begin to ask their own questions. "What if we used this shape instead...?" "What if I used odd numbers instead of even...?" "What if we used cubes instead of squares...?" "How can we be sure?" "What is the connection...?" and so on.

Leading to GCSE coursework ... and beyond

From 1991, coursework is a compulsory part of the GCSE mathematics examination, and *all* candidates have to undertake some extended coursework in order to meet the demands of the National Criteria. We do not feel that teachers or pupils should be asked to take on the preparation for this form of assessment without support, which is where this package comes in. It is vital that the later formal assessment is closely related to both the content and style of pupils' classroom experiences and that pupils practise the skills necessary for this assessment from the start of their secondary school career.

The investigations

The ideas that follow are designed to help some teachers to 'get started' and others to review their current practice. They are not intended to be the only approach for all teachers. As the investigations have been written with group or class presentation in mind, a number of questions need to be considered.

What preparation does the teacher need to make before starting?
Familiarity with the ideas and potential of the investigation will give you more confidence and make your responses to pupil comment and question all the richer. So start by working through the task yourself, if possible with a colleague. Make notes of things you encounter and any stumbling blocks you foresee. Think of the variety of resources that may be useful and have them available (though they need not be given out).

Should the lesson(s) have a structure?

Some may say that a structure prevents the natural development of pupils' ideas. However, many teachers know all too well the chaos that can ensue when no planning has been done. One possible model, appropriate to most of the investigations suggested, is as follows:

- Present the situation to the group or class and encourage, without judgement, all the ideas which arise. Note ideas as they come in. This may take as little as three minutes or as long as ten to twenty minutes.
- Let pupils, in pairs or individually, work on the problem for a while. (Ideally this should be at least ten minutes. They may need longer, but this can be judged on the basis of the progress you observe.)
- Bring the group or class together for a while to share any new findings or extensions of ideas already mentioned. At the end of this discussion you may decide that a further ten minutes or so working in pairs or individually would be productive.
- Ask the whole group or class: "What questions can you think of that could be asked about this problem?" Collect these questions on the board. The pupils now have available the experience of working on the problem with others or on their own, the recorded ideas that have been mentioned by others and a list of their questions.
- Get pupils back to working in pairs or individually, either continuing from where they left off or working on one of the questions identified above. (The time required for this stage will vary from group to group and from person to person.)

By this time the end of the first lesson will certainly have been reached, so decisions have to be made by you about homework or further lesson time.

A length of time to complete each task has not been suggested because this is influenced by many factors – the ability and interest of the group, your enthusiasm and inspiration, etc. However, pupils should be able to get something from each of the tasks in about an hour. A lesson of 35 minutes is not long enough to do justice to the open-ended nature of the activities, and some classes trialling the material spent a number of lessons on one investigation.

What is the teacher's role?

During the early stages of an investigation it is important that pupils' responses be listened to and valued. Where differences between pupils exist, use them to encourage further clarification and justification – this can help to develop more precise language and puts the onus of proving the 'correctness' on the pupils.

When pupils are working individually or in pairs, move around the classroom, observe pupils' actions and *listen* to their talk, ask for clarification, ask a question if you think it will help a pupil who is stuck. Above all be encouraging.

As you move around the classroom, ideas or questions may arise. You might like to write them on the board for future reference. When you get to the question-making time, don't be afraid to add your own – but don't let them dominate.

Simply getting some pupils to tell the others how they did it has disadvantages as well as advantages; you may prefer to ask those who have not progressed so far to explain what they were trying to do (which often helps them to sort out their own thinking) before letting others comment.

If you are introducing an investigation to a small group as opposed to a whole class you will need to modify some of the strategies. Use of the board may be inappropriate and the task will have to be paced so that pupils do the next part of the activity when the group is ready.

What should pupils be recording?

The request to do a 'write-up' has become the bane of many children's lives! So often they do the activity in the classroom with teacher support and are then asked to do the really difficult bit, the write-up, at home, on their own! This should be avoided, at least in the early stages. Anything that discourages pupils from working investigatively must be counter-productive.

Throughout the activity pupils should be encouraged to keep some kind of record of their findings, thoughts and conjectures. These recordings, which will probably need tidying up, can then form the main part of the write-up. Thus the written report develops as they go along. You may want to have a 'wholeness' to the written work and at least have a format of beginning, middle and end. The beginning may be something you do with them in the first half-an-hour of a lesson perhaps by saying: "Imagine you are having to explain to your friend in Australia how the activity started. How would you describe it to her?" Writing to some other person is a supportive way of getting pupils started on written reports of their work. The middle needs to be no more than a clear and ordered recording of the action, questions, conjectures and findings. The end may justify some of the things that have been said in the middle and can include other questions encountered but not necessarily tackled. Don't be in too much of a hurry to formalise the written work.

Sometimes you may feel that a formal write-up is not appropriate. Alternatives could include the production of a poster, a verbal report to the class, a booklet of ideas, or...

Display examples of pupil work in the classroom. Select good examples of all levels of ability. Any classroom display involving written text should be at pupils' eye-level.

The format of the investigations

The investigations in this book are presented in a standard format.

Text on the left-hand side of each page indicates what the pupils are expected to do, or questions they may be asked. Quotes have been used for teacher questions, though it is **not intended that these should be used verbatim**.

Text on the right-hand side of each page is a commentary on the more obvious or important aspects of what may happen. This part also includes ideas for the teacher, ways of working, and comments on the mathematics being developed.

At the end of some investigations there are ideas for possible ways of extending the activity. They are not, in general, to be used as a list to be worked through.

Miscellaneous notes

- Some basic information is provided at the start of the activity. This information is meant to be helpful, not prescriptive.
- The investigations may be used with a small group of pupils, or with a whole class.
- The term 'board' is used although many teachers use OHP and/or whiteboard. If working with a small group of pupils, the 'board' could be just a piece of paper on which ideas/results are written down.
- We have deliberately not supplied assessment material for the investigations. We feel that it is more important that pupils get a written or verbal *comment* on what they have done, rather than a mere mark or grade.
- The material is addressed to teachers, because we are aware that many teachers need to gain confidence with more open-ended work. One of the main skills for teachers to learn is when, and how, to intervene sensitively during an activity.
- Some investigations have a worksheet(s) for pupil use; this is indicated by a logo 🗋 next to the list of materials.
- The materials are designed in the first instance to give a balanced programme for first- and second-year pupils of all ability levels. It is not suggested that you do all the investigations with your pupils, or in the order that they occur in the book. However, the first few investigations are probably among the easiest, to get you started.
- We have used the term 'trial and improvement' to indicate the process by which pupils may explore a situation by trying out an initial idea, and then modifying their subsequent approaches or conjectures in the light of this initial experience.
- Any specific links to SMP 11–16 booklets are noted in the preamble, but each of the tasks can stand alone. And, of course, the investigations can be used whatever particular mathematics course is being followed.

Removing the structure

The presentation of the investigations is designed to promote confidence and success for teachers not familiar with more open-ended work. It is hoped that teachers will not see the structure as a strait-jacket but will feel free to use the investigations in as flexible a way as possible.

After using an investigation, notes could be made on the relevant pages to provide hints or information to make the task more successful next time. It is hoped that after a couple of attempts at an investigation the book's ideas could be dispensed with entirely.

This book is intended simply as a stepping stone from concentrating on content to a realisation that process is important. Investigations such as those here should not be seen as the end-point. It is intended that further materials will be produced leading towards the idea of an investigative approach.

There are many books and pamphlets available as sources of investigations; the problem is in filtering out those that will work for you. A short bibliography follows. It may be useful for you to select an investigation from one of these and then to prepare a lesson plan similar to those in this book.

A short bibliography

Points of Departure 1 and 2; *Investigation Cards*, Association of Teachers of Mathematics

Thinking Things Through, Leone Burton (Blackwell)

Mathematical Investigations in your Classroom, Dr S. Pirie (Macmillan Education)

Jump to It, *Leap to It*, *Race to It* and *Bounce to It*, Gillian Harsh (Manchester Polytechnic, School of Education, 799 Wilmslow Road, Didsbury, Manchester)

Investigations in Mathematics, Lorraine Mottershead (Blackwell)

Discovering Mathematics – The Art of Investigation, Tony Gardiner (Oxford Science Publications)

Mathematical Puzzling, Tony Gardiner (Oxford University Press)

Starting Points, Banwell, Saunders and Tahta (Tarquin Press)

Leapfrogs Books (Tarquin Press)

Thinking Mathematically, John Mason with Leone Burton and Kaye Stacey (Addison-Wesley)

A Way with Maths, N. Langdon and C. Snape (Cambridge University Press)

Mathematical Activities, *More Mathematical Activities* and *Even More Mathematical Activities*, Brian Bolt (Cambridge University Press)

The investigations

Consecutive sums

Materials Calculators could be made available – but not given out initially; plenty of rough paper.

Possible content and processes Simple whole-number arithmetic, prime numbers, multiples, factors, recognising rules and patterns, trial and improvement, organising data, predicting, checking, generalising.

Preamble Pupils are introduced to 'consecutive sums' through the idea that numbers can be made up from the sum of smaller numbers.

"Give me some (counting) numbers which add up to 5."

Keep a record on the board of all contributions.

"Are any of these sums the same?"

Discuss if, for example, 5 = 1 + 2 + 2 and 5 = 2 + 1 + 2 are different sums. The activity is more manageable if they are taken to be the same. This is assumed in what follows.

It is not essential to get all possible sums, but you will need to refer to 5 = 2 + 3 later!

"Write down as many ways as you can of making 6."

Pupils should work individually. Circulate and judge when to bring the class together.

Record contributions on the board. Allow pupils to make comments, or challenge contributions.

It is likely that all ten ways will be generated by the class.

You will need to refer to 6 = 1 + 2 + 3 shortly. You will have to decide what to do if this sum comes in another order. One way of dealing with this would be to agree with the class that all sums should have their numbers in ascending order.

Refer back to the sums for 5 and 6 on the board.
Underline 5 = 2 + 3 and 6 = 1 + 2 + 3.

"What is special about these sums?"

Accept all suggestions but focus on the idea of adding consecutive numbers.

Expect a variety of descriptions of the rule such as:

● *the numbers come after each other.*
● *the numbers are neighbours.*
● *the numbers are on the number line.*

The comments from other pupils should help to tighten up these descriptions. If the word 'consecutive' is mentioned by a pupil, it is important to make sure that everyone knows what it means. If it is not mentioned, then this is a good opportunity to introduce the word and clarify its meaning.

"Now find all possible consecutive sums for 9."

Record contributions on the board.

This should not take long as there are only two consecutive sums.
It is essential that the rule is well established before continuing. Find sums for other numbers if necessary, but be aware that some numbers (4 for example) have no consecutive sums.
For the remainder of the activity the pupils should work in pairs.

"Now choose some numbers of your own and find their consecutive sums. Keep your numbers small (less than 40?). See what you can find out."

Some pupils may tackle this activity simply by adding consecutive numbers, and seeing what totals they get.

Circulate and discuss problems as they arise. Do not direct pupils, but ask questions which will help their thinking and move them forward. Judge when to bring the class together.

Record results on the board. Discuss with the pupils anything they have discovered. Record this on the board also.

Pooling ideas in this way gives useful practice to pupils in explaining their thinking. It should also encourage listening, and responding, to others' explanations. It also helps in moving forward any pupils who have difficulty in generating their own ideas, or who feel that they have finished.

Encourage pupils to continue along any avenue which interests them, and to keep notes of their findings.

Pupils should be able to find a wide variety of patterns within this activity.
In discussions with pupils it may be appropriate to ask questions like:

- *Are there any numbers with no consecutive sums? If so, which ones are they?*
- *Is there anything special about the numbers with only one consecutive sum, two consecutive sums, three consecutive sums . . . ?*
- *Can you find any methods of predicting all the consecutive sums of a given number?*

> **Possible extensions**
> - What happens if you include 0 and negative numbers?
> - What happens if you use sums of consecutive even (or odd) numbers?

Corners on solids

Materials   Multilink (or similar) cubes, possibly triangular spotty paper.

Possible content and processes   Generalising and predicting, recording three-dimensional shapes.

Preamble   This activity aims to get pupils talking about and making three-dimensional shapes based on cubes. The task supports the work in the SMP 11–16 *Three dimensions* booklets.

Give each pupil five cubes.

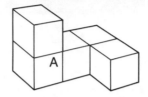

"Join your five cubes together. Only allow cubes to meet face to face."

"When you have made your shape, count how many corners it has."

> *Some pupils may need some guidance as to what constitutes a corner. It is crucial that this is established from the very outset.*
>
> *You need to decide whether 'inside corners' such as A are counted or not. The decision you make on this should not affect the development of the task.*

"Make some more shapes. Find the least number of corners."

"Can you do this in more than one way?"

> *At this point – depending on the group – it might be useful to encourage pupils to record their results in some way.*

"Find the greatest number of corners."

"Is there more than one shape with the largest possible number of corners?"

> *There should be plenty of experimentation and discussion. Allow this to continue as long it is productive before drawing the class together.*

Collect the results on the board. Encourage discussion and verification of the results.

"Find, by working in pairs, the smallest and largest numbers of corners using four or six cubes. Record the shapes which give these results."

Allow sufficient time for this. Now throw open the whole investigation.

"Try different numbers of cubes. Find the rule for the least number of corners."

"Is there a rule connecting the greatest number of corners with the number of cubes?"

"What sort of shapes have the least/most number of corners?"

There is plenty of scope here to encourage verbal description of three-dimensional solids.

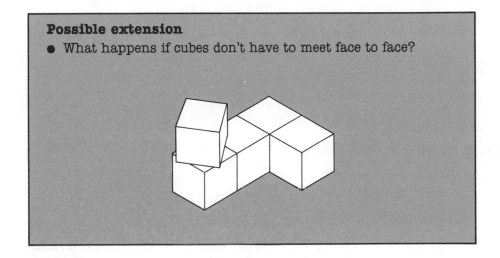

Possible extension

● What happens if cubes don't have to meet face to face?

4U + 1T

Materials	Possibly calculators.
Possible content and processes	Whole-number arithmetic.
Preamble	There is no obvious way of presenting this task in a concrete setting. Most pupils accept it as a piece of 'fun mathematics'.
	It is helpful to have pupils working in pairs or small groups to minimise arithmetical errors.

"Someone give me a two-digit number."

Write this on the board.

"Now I'm going to multiply the units digit by 4 and then add on the tens digit."

Do this and record the answer on the board.

> *The numbers 13, 26, 39 will generate themselves. The following text assumes that none of these was chosen.*

"I want you to do the same to this new number. What number do I get now?"

Repeat this a few times until all pupils have understood the rule for generation.

> *Only a few steps will be needed. Do not go on too long or you will form a loop. It is best for pupils to discover the loop for themselves.*

> *You may come across a single-digit number in this process. If you do not, then you should introduce one and discuss how to deal with it.*

"Choose a two-digit number of your own, and use this rule to make a chain of numbers. Watch what happens as your chain grows."

> *Depending on the group, this can be a suitable point to allow pupils to work on their own. Most pupils will be able to generate a chain without making arithmetical errors, but weaker ones may need help and/or a calculator.*

Circulate, help and prompt as appropriate.

After a short while, someone will notice that they have got back to a number they had before. When this happens, discuss it with the class.

> *It is important for pupils to realise that once a loop is formed, no new numbers are generated. They do not always find this obvious!*

"Will *all* numbers form loops?"

"How long are the loops? Are they the same length? Try other starting numbers."

Pupils should now work on their own. Many questions will arise in discussion with pupils. Those below are possible avenues of investigation.

- *How many starting numbers are there?*
- *How many loops are there?*
- *Can we show these chains in a drawing?*
- *Are there any self-generating numbers?*

Possible extensions

- There is nothing special about the 4, other than that it gives short chains. Change the 4 to some other number, so the rule is $aU + 1T$. Investigate what happens for different values of a.

  Investivate how many chains there are for each value of a and how long they are. Are there any values which give a single chain?

  Investigate self-generating numbers for different values of a.

  Extend even further by making the rule $aU + bT$ for different values of a and b.

  (*Note*. For some values of a and b the chains get quite long. You might encourage pupils to write a short computer program to perform the calculations.)

- How would you extend the activity to three-digit numbers?

Splitting numbers

Materials   Calculators.

**Possible content
and processes**   Simple whole-number arithmetic with a possible extension to decimals.

"Give me some whole numbers which add up to 11."

Write these numbers on the board. $5 + 6 = 11$

"What do we get when we multiply these numbers together?" $5 \times 6 = 30$

"Give me some more numbers which add up to 11." $2 + 2 + 7 = 11$

"What do we get when we multiply these numbers together?" $2 \times 2 \times 7 = 28$

The number of examples needed to get the general idea that we first express 11 as a sum and then multiply the 'bits' will depend on the group in question.
There is no restriction on the number of 'bits'.

"See if you can find another set of numbers which add up to 11, but which give a greater product than we have got so far. You can use as many numbers as you like, so long as they add up to 11."

"Try to find the biggest product there is."

This is best done by pupils working on their own for about ten minutes, then with the teacher drawing the group together.

"Does it make any difference how many bits you split 11 into or how big the bits are?"

"Do you get a bigger result on the whole when you split 11 up into three bits or two bits? Which is better, small bits or big bits?

In general, small bits tend to increase the product. For example, 5 can be replaced by 2 + 3 which increases the product.
Bits of size 1 obviously contribute nothing to the product.
Part of the problem is to look at whether you use 2s or 3s – for example, is it better to replace 6 by 2 + 2 + 2 or 3 + 3?

The whole activity will be devalued if pupils are simply told the largest number and then set the problem of finding the bits which give this number. The whole investigation should now be thrown open.

"Work together in twos or threes. Choose some numbers of your own, but keep them less than 20 to start with. Find the largest product in each case. See what you can find out. Write down anything you notice."

Circulate amongst the groups. Encourage them to note down any patterns or findings. You may like to use these as discussion points later on.

When you think they have had sufficient time to explore at least two or three numbers, draw the group together.

"Has anyone noticed anything about the sort of numbers (bits) that give the largest product?"

Generally speaking, pupils will say things like (a) the numbers are close together (e.g. 3s and 2s or 3s and 4s) or (b) they are nearly all 3s. Encourage them to expand on these conjectures and to give you examples. (Record them on the board – the number, the bits and the product.) When you have fully discussed the ideas, . . .

"I would like you to find the largest products for all the numbers from 1 to 20 and to record them in a table. You may wish to use some of the ideas we have just discussed to help you find the largest product a little quicker than before."

At this stage it is advisable to move each group forward as and when they are ready. Determine this by getting them to talk to you about their table of results.

One possible way forward is to present them with one or two numbers much larger than 20 (but less than 50) and see if they can then apply their acquired knowledge and understanding.
*   Later ask them to explain the largest product for both 50 and 51! Why?*

If they can master this, ask them to see if there are any patterns to be found in the sequence of largest products. Is it possible, for example, to predict the largest product for 21, 22, 23, without first breaking each number into bits?

> **Possible extension**
> ● Suppose you are allowed to use decimals, as well as, or instead of, whole numbers. Is it possible to obtain a larger product? If so, what is it?
>
> More able pupils may have considered this possibility at an earlier stage.

Arranging tables

Materials	Squared paper, scissors.
Possible content and processes	Number patterns, generalising, predicting.
Preamble	Rectangular tables are involved in this activity so it could be introduced practically, although in the following it is assumed that this is not the case.

Draw a diagram like this.

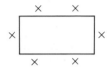

"This diagram represents a table and six seats. Suppose I wish to put two tables together so that they seat more than six people. How can I do it?"

Record all suggestions.

Establish that there needs to be some rules about which arrangements are allowed.

It is more manageable if the rules only allow the arrangements shown here.

Continue accepting suggestions until all three of the arrangements have emerged.

Draw each accepted arrangement on the board.

"How many seats are there for each of these arrangements?"

There may well be some discussion about whether the 'L' arrangements will seat nine or ten. It is important that it is established that it is in fact nine.

"What is the largest and smallest number of seats we have found for two tables?"

Write the number beside each relevant diagram.

"Work together in twos or threes, and try to find the largest and smallest number of seats for arrangements of three tables."

Some pupils may need to cut out 2 × 1 rectangles and manipulate them.

Some interesting debates may ensue about how many seats 'L' arrangements have.

Judge when to bring the class together to establish the largest and smallest number of seats.

"What about four tables?"

"What about other numbers of tables?"

"Find a way to predict the largest and smallest number of seats for 20 tables."

Some pupils may make a table of their results, others may approach the problem spatially. The formulas s = 4 + 2t (smallest) and s = 2 + 4t (largest) may emerge, either formally or informally. However, it would be a mistake to force the pace or regard these as an end-point for all pupils.

A whole-class discussion may be valuable.

Possible extensions
- Repeat the investigation with different sized rectangular tables, for example 3 × 1, 4 × 2.
- Repeat the investigation with pupils' own designs of tables, for example, half-hexagonal.

Hair

Materials Heads! Children might also require other 'props' such as rubber bands, rulers, tape measures, string, etc.

Possible content and processes Counting, methods of estimation, whole-number arithmetic, sampling.

Preamble This is a practical activity for younger secondary children. It should be seen as one of a number of estimating activities. However, if you feel this activity is too personal for some children, estimating blades of grass in a given area of lawn would be an alternative starting point.

Arrange your class in groups of three or four before you start.

"How many hairs have you got on your head? Work in your groups to estimate the number. I suggest you get an estimate for one of your group."

This will generate lively activity, usually short-lived. A wide variety of numbers will quickly be produced. Decide when to stop the activity.

Ask someone from each group to describe their method.

Encourage others to respond, but react impartially. Pupils' responses are usually variations of: find the number per unit area and then work out the total area.

"Use some of these suggestions in your group to estimate the number of hairs on the head of another member of your group".

Collect the results from each group and allow whatever discussion seems necessary.

Possible extensions

- Library research: how many hairs are there on the human head? What sort of variation might be expected? Different references may give different values: about a million (The Hutchinson Encyclopaedia); about a hundred thousand (Readers Digest Book of Facts).
- A class discussion on the comparison between the answers obtained and the 'research' answer might be conducted.
- Other estimation activities could include:
    How long does it take to count to a million?
    How many bricks in a wall?
    How many pores on the body?
    How many blades of grass on a lawn?

Chess

Materials   Chessboard, squared paper, tracing paper. Possibly isometric or triangular spotty paper.

Possible content and processes   Square numbers, pattern spotting.

Preamble   This is a fairly closed investigation. This activity links in with SMP 11–16 *Squaring and cubing* or 3b *Squares and cubes*.

Write 'CHESS' on the board.

"Who plays chess?"

Ask one pupil to describe a chessboard to the rest of the class.
Draw this on the board.

> *It can be helpful to draw the square board, but then discuss further before drawing the divisions. It is not necessary to shade the squares. This part of the activity is not essential, but will develop pupils' descriptive powers and will bring out the existence of the 'outside' square.*

"How many squares are there on a chessboard?"

> *The first answers are usually '64'. Someone will suggest '65'.*

Discuss the suggestions with the class. Refer to your drawing.

> *From this it will emerge that squares of different sizes can be found. Make sure that all pupils are aware of the range of different sizes, but do not give too much away about how to find them.*

"Now see if you can answer my question about the number of squares."

Circulate and discuss problems as they arise.

> *There will be much haphazard work at finding squares. Do not intervene too quickly.*

> *When counting, many pupils will not allow squares to overlap and will only find 16 of the 2 × 2 squares. They cannot manage 3 × 3 squares as they 'don't fit' . . . This will highlight the need for overlaps.*

> *To help with the mechanics of counting, some pupils may find it useful to make tracings of 2 × 2, 3 × 3, . . . , squares to slide around the board.*

> *Some pupils might find it helpful to start on a smaller board first.*

> *Encourage tabulation of the numbers of each size of square. Very few spot that the sequence is of square numbers. This needs to be brought out if pupils are to attempt the extensions.*

> *A whole-class discussion at the end is valuable.*

Possible extensions

- How many squares are there on an $m \times m$ board, on an $m \times n$ board?
- How many rectangles are there on an $m \times m$ board, on an $m \times n$ board?
- How many cubes are there in a $3 \times 3 \times 3$ cube? ... a $4 \times 4 \times 4$ cube? ... an $n \times n \times n$ cube?

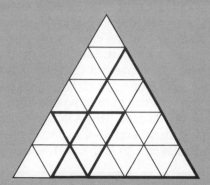

Size 5

- How many triangles are there in this diagram? (Some have been emphasised to help.)
  What if the big triangle is of size 3, or size 6 or ...?
- What about other shapes?

Sheep pens

Materials   1 cm square spotty paper for pupils' use; possibly 1 cm spotty OHP master copy; a box of drinking straws (enough for 10 straws each); a dozen 30 cm rulers (or sticks); 36 cubes or counters.

Possible content and processes   Area, pattern searching, tabulating, conjecturing, generalising.

Preamble   This activity supports the work of SMP 11–16 level 4(b) *Area 3*.

It is a good idea to make your introduction 'large scale', that is using an area of the classroom floor to represent a farmer's field, the 30 cm rulers (or sticks) to represent the hurdles and cubes (or counters) to represent the position of the posts. Make a 6 × 6 square array on the floor (with the cubes or counters) and begin by having the pupils sitting/standing around the array.

The pupils each need a maximum of 20 straws. This is obtained by cutting the 10 straws into half. This can be done before the lesson, or the pupils can do it themselves before they start the investigation.

"Imagine that the rulers (sticks) represent sheep hurdles and the floor represents a farmer's field."

Make sure that the pupils know what a sheep hurdle is.

"The farmer has purchased a number of these hurdles and decides to experiment with different shapes of sheep pen. The hurdles can be joined together in two ways like this." (Demonstrate.)

——— • ———   or   ——— •

"The cubes (counters) represent the places where the posts could go. Imagine that the farmer starts off with, say, twelve hurdles and begins to look at the various possibilities."

Hand the twelve 'hurdles' to one pupil.

"Make a sheep pen using all twelve hurdles."

On completion, ask: "How many squares have you enclosed?"

Record on the board the shape and the number of squares enclosed.

Collect up the hurdles and hand them to another pupil.

"Make me a different sheep pen."

At this stage, or later, the question of what is meant by 'different' may arise.

"How many squares have been enclosed this time?"

Record on the board the shape and the number of squares enclosed.

Repeat the process once more.

"It looks as though there may be several possibilities. Work in small groups and try to find all the different possible shapes of pen you can make with 12 hurdles. For each one, record its shape and the number of squares enclosed. However, each group must come up with *one set of agreed results*, so before starting you might like to discuss how you are going to share out the work load."

Give out the spotty paper and six straws to each pupil.

*If the straws have not been cut in half before the lesson, ask pupils to do it now. This then enables them to have 12 hurdles. Although the pupils can work individually within the group, they have to combine and compare in order to come up with **one set of agreed results**.*

At an appropriate time . . .

"What is the largest area and what is the smallest area you can enclose, in terms of the number of squares?"

Establish that these are 9 and 5 respectively.

Record these results.

"What if I had used a different number of hurdles? What would be the largest and smallest areas then? Work in your small groups. Don't use more than 20 hurdles. Remember that each group has to come up with *one set of agreed results*. See if you can find a relationship between the number of hurdles and the largest and smallest areas you can enclose."

Circulate and judge when to draw the class together.

"We need to sort out all the results. How could we do this?"

Accept all contributions and discuss. A table of results (number of hurdles [in order], largest area, smallest area) will enable you to discuss patterns, make predictions, etc.

"Is it possible to predict what the largest and smallest areas would be for, say, 50 hurdles or 100 hurdles?"

You may also like to ask why no-one has come up with an odd number of hurdles.

The relationship between the number of hurdles and the smallest area is quite straightforward. However, for the largest areas there is one rule if the number of hurdles is a multiple of 4 (e.g. 100) and another if not (e.g. 50). Why?

Arithmogons

Materials   Arithmogon worksheet (optional).

Possible content and processes   Simple whole-number arithmetic. Possibly decimals, fractions, negative numbers and simultaneous equations. Organising data, trial and improvement, predicting and generalising.

Preamble   This activity may at first appear to be a simple puzzle to solve. Many pupils do not find the next examples easy. Additional problems are not apparent until quite a few arithmogons have been tried and there is some data to work on.

Draw a few blank arithmogons on the board.

Put these numbers in the boxes of one of them.

"Here is an arithmogon. The number in each box is the sum of the numbers to be put in the two circles on either side."

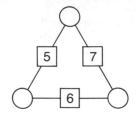

"What numbers should go in the circles?"

> *The numbers 5, 6, 7 have been deliberately chosen as consecutive numbers. You will quickly get a correct solution.*
>
> *Ensure that all the group understand what is required.*

"Now work in pairs and try these."

> *Give them about four examples. These should have consecutive odd–even–odd numbers in the boxes: e.g. 15, 16, 17; 23, 24, 25; 47, 48, 49; 63, 64, 65 (some clockwise, some anti-clockwise). These particular examples are straightforward and should give pupils confidence in handling the rules.*
>
> *Judge when to bring the class back together.*

"What are your solutions?"

Write them on the board and get the class to agree when they are correct.

> *At this stage, you may wish to draw out the strategies that pupils have used to solve the problems.*
>
> *Be aware that some properties of the examples so far will not apply to the more general problem to be developed now.*

Draw a new empty arithmogon on the board.

"Now give me three numbers to go in the boxes of this arithmogon. This time let's not have consecutive numbers."

> *You may need to explain the word 'consecutive'.*

"Let's try to find the 'circle' numbers for this arithmogon.".

Accept ideas and get the group to use the suggestions made to 'home-in' on the answer.

You may become involved in halves and, if the sum of the two smaller numbers is less than the largest number, negative numbers.

"What numbers shall we put in the boxes for these three arithmogons?"

Put these on the board.

"Try to find the circle numbers for these arithmogons in your pairs."

"When you have solved these, set each other arithmogons to solve."

Methods will begin to emerge and pupils should be encouraged to record these alongside their diagrams. Questions will arise, or should be encouraged, to determine when:

● *fractions are needed*
● *negative numbers arise*
● *answers can be predicted from the numbers in the boxes.*

You may like to encourage some pupils to use algebra if or when appropriate.

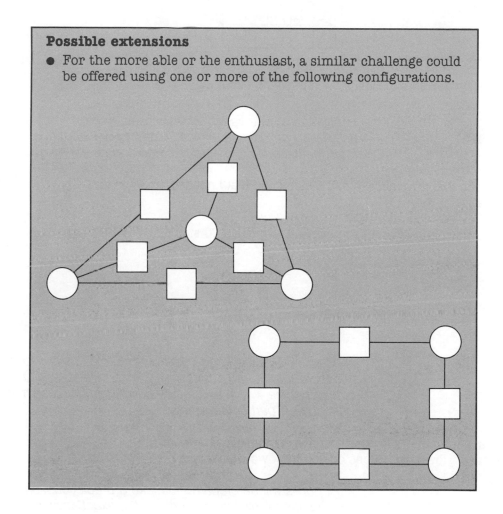

Possible extensions
● For the more able or the enthusiast, a similar challenge could be offered using one or more of the following configurations.

Building steps

Materials	Cubes (e.g. Multilink or centicubes) – about 50 cubes per pair or group. Calculators to be available.
Possible content and processes	Whole-number arithmetic: even, odd, triangular, square numbers, consecutive numbers. Trial and improvement, recognising number patterns, organising data, predicting, checking, generalising.
Preamble	Initially this activity involves pupils predicting and checking, and the emphasis is on oral work (explaining, listening, discussing).

Using cubes – from a bag of about 50 – make this shape and show it to the class.

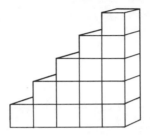

"I've made a staircase shape. What can you tell me about my staircase?"

> *Encourage a wide variety of responses, accepting all contributions and giving pupils time to think. Begin to draw out from the pupils the facts that your staircase has 5 steps and needs 15 cubes.*

"We have agreed that my staircase has 5 steps and that I needed 15 cubes to make it."

"Do you think I have enough cubes in this bag to make a 20-step staircase?"

Take a yes/no vote.

Give each pair or group of pupils approximately 50 cubes to check their prediction.

> *Let pupils build their 'largest staircase'. Some pupils will have no doubt that there are too few cubes for a 20-step staircase (it needs 210 cubes) but the way in which they build their staircase may help them with the next part of the activity.*

"We agree that each pair/group does not have enough cubes to make a 20-step staircase. How many cubes do you think we would need?"

> *Most pupils will be prepared to make a prediction; some pupils may feel that they know how to work out the exact answer.*

Record all suggestions on the board (for later use).

"We want to check these suggestions. Work in pairs and use *your* cubes to help you. Calculators are available. Keep notes on what you do so that you can explain how you arrived at your answer."

Give pupils time to tackle the problem. Move around the room and interact as seems appropriate, but don't direct. Keep a note of interesting approaches.

Some pupils will arrive at an answer very quickly, although it may not be the correct one. For example, a common 'mistake' is to predict that if a 5-step staircase needs 15 cubes, then a 20-step staircase will need 4 × 15 cubes.

Try to react impartially to methods and answers so that pupils will be willing to describe to the rest of the class what they have done.

Judge when to draw the class together to share and discuss ideas.

Refer to each of the suggested answers on the board.

"Who agrees with this?"

Invite explanations of methods and answers.

You may wish to invite some pupils to use the board.

Encourage other pupils to ask for clarification, to make comments and to challenge methods and answers.

For pupils to appreciate the need for clear explanation and 'active' listening you will need to:
- *react impartially to answers and explanations*
- *encourage **them** to comment on and challenge what others say*
- *make it necessary for them to justify the statements they make.*

Make sure that all the different answers and methods are given an airing (draw on anything you noted earlier).

It is highly likely that by the time all contributions and challenges have been made, there will be agreement that 210 cubes are needed to make a 20-step staircase.

Possible extensions
- How many cubes will be needed for 25, 40, 65, 100 steps?
- Find a general rule for any number of steps.
- Finding quick methods for adding consecutive numbers.
- What happens if other shapes of staircase are used, such as the following?

Badges

Materials 1 cm or 2 cm squared paper, pencils, rulers, coloured pens, coloured chalk.

Possible content and processes Simple ideas of combinations, organisation of pictorial data to facilitate counting, generalising and predicting.

Preamble A drawing and counting activity. The 'obvious' strategy of merely 'drawing all possible badges' must at some stage be refined by grouping the badges in some systematic way.

Draw several five-cell badges like this one on the board.

"A youth club has decided that each member should have a badge shaped like this. The coloured pattern on each badge must be different. Each square can be coloured red, yellow or blue, but the members don't want two red (or two blue, or two yellow) squares alongside each other. They don't mind if, say, two reds touch at a corner."

Ask a pupil to colour in one of your diagrams.

"Is this colouring allowed?"

Ask pupils to colour other badges until the rules for colouring are understood.

"Are they all different?"

Various questions may arise here or later:
"Are reflections different?" (Yes!)
"Do you have to use all three colours each time?" (No!)

Encourage pupils to work in pairs (threes? fours?) to answer these questions:

"Could we make enough different badges for everyone in our class (year? school?) to have a different badge?"

"How many different badges do you think there are altogether?"

Give plenty of time for pupils to get into the problem. During this period, be very sparing with prompts.

First approaches will be based largely on drawing. Those who begin to be troubled by unintentional repeats, or by the number of drawings, might be asked:
- *How will you know when you have got them all?*
- *How can you avoid repeats?*
- *Is there some way of grouping your badges which might help you keep track?*

Look out for, and encourage, partially systematic approaches such as attempts to start by drawing all possible badges with blue in the middle of the top row. Get pupils to state explicitly what they are doing and encourage them to follow it through. You may wish to ask explicitly:

"Suppose there are 20 badges with blue in the middle of the top row. How many do you think there would be with yellow in the middle of the top row? How many would there be with red?"

It is hoped that eventually pupils will realise things like:

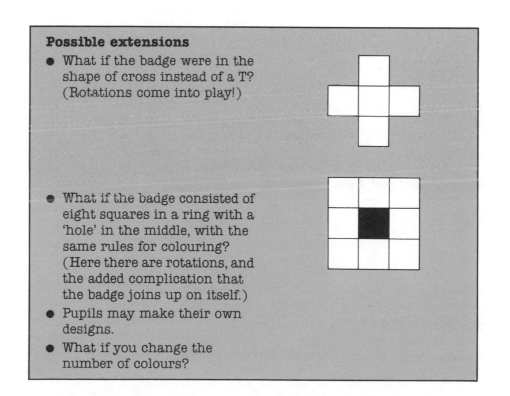

and

Other strategies may be equally valid.

Possible extensions
- What if the badge were in the shape of cross instead of a T? (Rotations come into play!)

- What if the badge consisted of eight squares in a ring with a 'hole' in the middle, with the same rules for colouring? (Here there are rotations, and the added complication that the badge joins up on itself.)
- Pupils may make their own designs.
- What if you change the number of colours?

Necklaces

Materials	Plain paper.
Possible content and processes	Tabulation, proof by exhaustion, modulo arithmetic.
Preamble	An investigation which pupils of all abilities can usefully tackle. It is important for pupils to take care with the numbers; the arithmetic is simple but it is easy to make mistakes.

"I'm going to start with two numbers, 1 and 3, and use them as starting numbers to produce a number chain. I have a rule that I want you to find."

$$1 \nearrow 3 \nearrow$$

"Try to see how I get the next number each time."

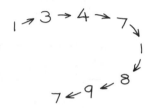

Don't draw the chain in a straight line.

The calculations (addition modulo 10) can be done very quickly just by adding and ignoring the tens digit. But go slowly! The purpose is to give pupils time to search for rules and to test each rule to see if it really works. Don't go further than is shown here.

"What do you think the rule is?"

Accept each suggested rule, asking for clarification if necessary. For each suggested rule, ask the class to judge whether or not it fits the facts so far.

"In a moment I am going to write down the next two numbers. First I want you to write down what you think they will be."

Then fill in the next two numbers.

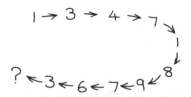

Continue the discussion until the rule is well established.

"Now copy this chain and continue it. See what happens if you keep going."

Give them plenty of time to get past the place where the chain repeats.

"What have you noticed about the numbers in the chain?"

Some pupils will have failed to notice that the chain repeats, or will have made errors in their working.

"Start a new chain with a different pair of numbers."

Watch out for errors.
Be aware that some chains are very long (e.g. 3 → 1 has 60 elements).

Apart from the simple (but very real) pleasure of generating numbers recursively, and the important lesson of accuracy, one would also like pupils to analyse the problem mathematically.

"Can you say, without working it out, what happens when you start with 1 and 8?"

"How many different chains/necklaces are there?"

"How can you be sure when you have them all?"

"How many different 'beads' and 'links' are there altogether in *all* of the necklaces?"

One approach to help pupils answer such questions is to consider all possible starting pairs. Pupils could draw up a table of pairs and tick off those in the chains they have done.

Possible extensions

- What happens if you work out necklaces modulo 5 instead of modulo 10? Or modulo 9? Or modulo 11? Or...?
  (There is lots of mileage in this. For example, compare what happens modulo 10 with what happens modulo 5 and modulo 2. Or compare what happens modulo 6 with modulo 2 and modulo 3.)

- What happens if you use the same kind of adding rule modulo 10 but start with letters a and b instead of with numbers? Thus ... → $4a + 5b$ → $5a + 9b$ → $9a + 4b$ → ...

Surrounds

Materials Cubes (Multilink or centicubes) or square tiles – about 50 cubes per pair or group of pupils (consider carefully the distribution of colours). 1 cm squared paper, coloured felt-tip pens or crayons.

Possible content and processes Spatial, number patterns, generalising.

Preamble This activity extends the work in SMP 11–16 level 2(b) *Discovering rules*.

"I want each of you to use three cubes of the same colour to make a shape like this."

"Place your shape on the table. Now use cubes of a different colour to surround your shape."

As you move around the classroom you are likely to find that the word 'surround' has been interpreted in different ways:

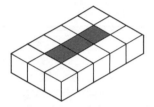

Bring the class together and encourage pupils to describe their different ways of *surrounding*.

You can pursue any or all of these examples. To enable the class to continue discussing the problem, you may choose to restrict it to one of these. The following example has been chosen here.

"Make sure you all have this shape in front of you."

"How many cubes do you need for this *surround*?"

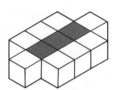

"Now *surround* your shape in this way again, using a new colour."

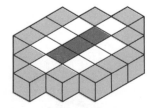

You will need to check that the new shape maintains the pattern. Pupils could be encouraged to record each stage on squared paper.

"How many cubes did you need this time?"

"How many cubes do you think you would need to *surround* the shape again?"

"Check your guess."

If you are short of cubes, get the pupils to work in pairs or groups at this stage.

"Is there any way you can decide on the number of cubes needed to continue making *surrounds*?"

Some time should be available to pursue this question. You must decide when it is time to collect results on the board. Relating the number of cubes needed each time with the 'order of surrounds' – 1st surround, 8 cubes; 2nd surround, 12 cubes; 3rd surround, 16 cubes; etc. – will make it possible to ask some pupils, "How many cubes will you need for the 10th surround, 20th surround, 40th surround? . . ." Some focus on the connection between the 'surround' number and the 'number of cubes' should be made.

Possible extensions

You can now allow pupils to take up any of the questions they have raised, or set the next task(s) yourself. Having decided whether pupils will work individually, in pairs or as groups, it is only necessary to start the class off with these new activities. Questions are more usefully asked as they work.

● Start the activity with some different shapes.

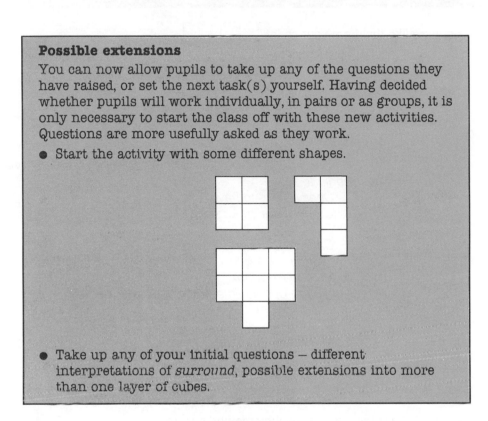

● Take up any of your initial questions – different interpretations of *surround*, possible extensions into more than one layer of cubes.

Box-ing

Materials 2 cm squared paper (at least two sheets per pupil), scissors.

Possible content and processes Spatial awareness, nets, verbalising.

Preamble Have one 3 × 3 square already cut out. The activity involves visualising and making nets which will fold up to make a box. Pupils should not add tabs or attempt to stick the boxes together with glue or sticky tape. It is recommended that this activity should not be done while work on the booklets *Three dimensions 1* or *2* is in progress.

"Cut out a 3 × 3 square like this from your sheet."

When they have all done this . . .

"Make me a box."

Be prepared for puzzled looks . . . but given time, the questions will begin to flow:
"Does it have to have a lid?"
"Can you cut squares off?"
"Can you fold it?"
"Can you cut along the lines?"
Answer all such queries with, "Do whatever you think is necessary in order to make a box."
At the appropriate time, when you know the majority have made a box (the open cube), . . .

Select a pupil who has made a box and ask them to explain their method to the rest of the class.

"Has anyone used a different method?"

Select a pupil who has and ask them to explain their method and why it is different from the previous one.

"Are there any other ways?"

Again, ask for an explanation of the method and how it differs.

"There seem to be several different methods. How many different methods can you find altogether? Work in groups of three or four in order to share your ideas and the work. You will need to think carefully about how you are going to record the different methods."

It is possible to make the open cube box

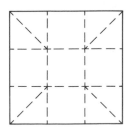

● *without doing any cutting at all*

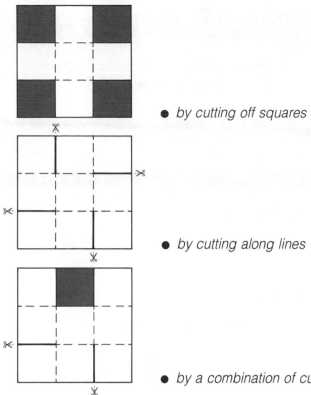

● *by cutting off squares*

● *by cutting along lines*

● *by a combination of cutting along lines and cutting off squares*

● *...*

If, for example, four squares are removed, ask them how many ways they could do this to give the net of a box. Give them plenty of time and then judge when to bring the class together.

Spend some time discussing the different methods and the ways of recording them.

A display of all the results can be helpful. Stick bases of the boxes onto a large sheet of paper or card, leaving the other faces free.

It may be appropriate to stop the activity here. Some pupils may have discovered that it is possible to make the open cube box from a 3 × 2 rectangle. If this has not been found, you could ask:

"I started with a 3 × 3 square which is made up of 9 unit squares. Is it possible to start with fewer unit squares, either as a rectangle or a square, and still be able to make the open cube box?"

Possible extensions

● What is the smallest square or rectangle you can start with and make a closed cube (a cube with a lid)?

● What is the smallest rectangle or square you can start with and make a 1 × 1 × 2 cuboid?

● Investigate ways of making tetrahedra from 2 cm isometric paper.

Digital sums

Materials Calculators available if needed.

Possible content and processes Whole-number arithmetic, generalising, divisibility tests.

Preamble Pupils may already have had experience in finding digital sums. For this activity, start by establishing that everyone knows what is meant by 'digital sum'.

"Someone give me a seven-digit number." (Say 5426783.)

Defining the word 'digit' may well not be necessary – there is usually someone who knows or is willing to make a guess.

"What is the sum of its digits – what do the digits add up to?"

Write this on the board: $5426783 \rightarrow 35$ $(5 + 4 + 2 + 6 + 7 + 8 + 3 = 35.)$

Now do the same with 35.
$35 \rightarrow 8$ $(3 + 5 = 8)$

"We shall say that 5426783 has *digital sum* 8."

Try some other large numbers of, say, five, six or seven digits. Establish the understanding of digital sum and, either from a pupil's example or one of your own, draw attention to one with a digital sum of 9.

*When recording these, record the whole chain
$75978 \rightarrow 36 \rightarrow 9$.*

"Find another number with a digital sum of 9. Give me the chain for your number."

Note the chains given for several of the pupils' numbers. Ask pupils to record them for later use.

"Work in pairs and find out all you can about numbers having a digital sum of 9. It may help to use a calculator."

As you move around the class, you will find some pupils who are not able to work with large numbers. Ask them to give you small numbers with a digital sum of 9 – collecting all the numbers less than 100 with the digital sum of 9 should help!

The fact that all the numbers are multiples of 9 will be noticed by some – suggest they keep it a secret for a while to give others the opportunity to discover this – some may notice that the two-digit numbers in the chains are multiples of 9.

Now the pupils have discovered a relationship between the digital sum and the starting number, the activity could be pursued in at least the following two ways:

- *Does a similar relationship hold for other digital sums? For example, consider a starting number which does not have a digital sum of 9, such as $3496 \rightarrow 22 \rightarrow 4$. Are all starting numbers with a digital sum of 4, multiples of 4? Try other digital sums.*
- *Write a list of multiples of any number, e.g. 4: 4, 8, 12, 16, 20, . . . Find their digital sums. Investigate any patterns.*

Number and patterns

Materials Worksheets (2). Initially at least one copy of worksheet 1 per pupil.

Possible content and processes Simple number work. Recognising number patterns, predicting, verbalising.

Preamble This activity is to encourage pupils to talk about numbers and patterns, and is not an investigation of Pascal's triangle.

Write on the board: 2, 3, 5, __, __

"What could come next?"

"Write down what you think the next two numbers could be. Make sure you have a good reason for your answers."

Ask a pupil for their numbers – note them on the board in the spaces.

"Has anyone else got these numbers?"

Get the pupils to describe all their different reasons.

"Has anyone got different numbers?" Ask for reasons for these.

> *The purpose of this is to make the point that different numbers or different reasons can be equally valid.*

Give each pupil a copy of worksheet 1.

"Look for patterns of numbers on the worksheet. Put in as many numbers as you can, keeping to your patterns. There may be more than one way to do this."

> *For this initial part of the activity try to limit pupil–pupil interaction and avoid any direct involvement yourself. Questions should be met with a response like "It's what you think that counts, as long as you are happy that it fits your patterns."*
>
> *Judge when to move on.*

"Now work in pairs. Take it in turns to pick a line – vertical, horizontal or diagonal – and explain to your partner how the pattern was made."

"You and your partner may have different number patterns. There is nothing wrong with that so long as your reasons work for every case."

> *Whilst this is going on, it may be useful to assume the role of umpire. Pupils should be encouraged to add to their sheets in the light of this activity. The whole activity could be turned into a game, one point for a horizontal or vertical line and two for a slanting line.*
>
> *Judge when to draw the class together to pool their ideas and results.*

Give out worksheet 2.
"This one starts differently. Fill in as many as you can. Try to find your own patterns."

Number cells

Materials   Squared paper – centimetre is useful.

Possible content   Number bonds, addition and subtraction, and the possibility of
and processes   decimals, fractions, negative numbers and algebraic expressions.
Organising data, trial and improvement, predicting and generalising.

Draw a 5-cell rectangle on the board.

"Give me a number to go in the first cell."

12				

"Now give me a number for the second cell."

12	7			

Accept numbers larger or smaller than the first number.

Complete the five cells by adding consecutive pairs without telling the
pupils your rule.

12	7	19	26	45

"Can you see what I am doing?"

Repeat this with several more 5-cell rectangles in this way until the rule
of adding consecutive pairs is well established.

*Avoid agreeing with, or rejecting, the explanations offered by pupils.
Use your responses to encourage all pupils to keep thinking. Finally,
ask someone to explain the 'rule'. This can help both the 'explainer'
and any pupils who are still in doubt.*

Draw another 5-cell rectangle.

"Give me a number to put in the first cell."

Now *you* (teacher) put a number in the last cell.

5				28

*To make the next challenge relatively easy, make sure that the sum of
the first and last numbers is a multiple of 3 (you can work out why
yourself!). It will help if the last number is significantly larger than the
first.*

"See if you can fill in the three empty cells, using the same rule as
before."

Encourage trial and improvement and ask the pupils to explain why
they chose their numbers.

Give pupils plenty of time – for those who finish this particular
challenge, invite them to choose the first and last numbers for
themselves. Try several more examples for the class where you invite
the first number and place the last number yourself – don't forget to
make their sum a multiple of three!

It does appear that the challenge to fill in the three squares does distract some pupils from the original rule. Other pupils will usually correct this without teacher intervention. When everyone has had a reasonable go and most have tasted success, move on to ask:

"How are you solving these? Is there a method you can describe to others?"

The most likely kind of response is: "First make a guess at the number in the second square. If this produces a last square which is too big, try again with a smaller number in the second square." Don't be surprised if some come up with more sophisticated methods – even the reason why the first and last numbers add to a multiple of 3. When pupils seem happy with filling in the three middle squares, move on.

Try the following on some new 5-cell drawings.
"Give me a number for the first cell; give me a number for the last cell.
Find the numbers for the other three cells."
Repeat this process.

It is likely that the pupils will choose examples where the sum of the first and last numbers is a multiple of 3. If this happens include one of your own where this is not the case.

Most pupils will still use 'trial and improvement'. Some will claim that the awkward ones can't be done. Others will explain that "If I try 2 (say) in the second square, the last number is too small, and if I try 3 in the second square the last number is too big." It may then be more appropriate to ask: "Well, what number in the second square would you expect to work exactly?" Pupils often suggest $2\frac{1}{2}$ (2.5). If so, then this should be pursued on the basis of what they know; this is not the time to stop the activity and teach, or revise, fractions and decimals (though you may wish to take note of what will need attention at a later date).

If it seems there is a need, at any stage, to stop the class activity and move into pairs, then do so, with each pupil setting a challenge for their partner.

An example like this | 13 | | | | 20 | *will raise the need*

for negative numbers. Although manipulation of negative numbers may not be in the pupils' experience, it does seem that the suggestion of 'minus numbers' is a natural response.

Depending on the group the question can be asked:

"If I write down the 'first' and 'last' number for any 5-cell rectangle, find a rule which gives the second number."

> **Possible extensions**
> - What happens if you have a different number of cells to start with? Is there a rule for an *n*-cell rectangle?
> - Explore what happens if you invent a new rule for moving from cell to cell. Try multiplying pairs, differencing pairs,...

Fibonacci (in reverse)

Materials Squared paper, calculators.

Possible content and processes Addition, subtraction, division (possibly), estimating.

Preamble This activity is best suited to a group of above-average pupils. It is necessary for the pupils to have experience of 'Fibonacci-type' number sequences. Spend a few minutes at the start of the lesson reminding the pupils of these. It may help to have done the 'Number cells' task first. For the body of this task only positive numbers will be used.

"See if you can find a 'Fibonacci type' sequence of which 50 is a member but is not the first or the second term."

Give the pupils a few minutes to work on this. When you think they are ready, collect half a dozen or so different examples and write them on the board.

Often the examples you collect will contain only two terms in front of the 50. The examples given can usually be further extended to the left. For example 22, 28, 50 can be extended to 16, 6, 22, 28, 50.

"Is it possible to extend any of the examples further to the left?"

It is crucial that they realise this is often possible before moving on.

"What is the largest number of terms you can get before the 50?"

This may take longer than you think.

It is possible to get six terms preceding the 50. Obviously the 'key number' is the one you choose to put directly before the 50.

Judge when to bring the class together. Check the longest chain suggested. If the key number suggested is not 31, tell them there is a better solution and ask them to find it.

When they have the correct solution tell them you will use the term 'key number' for this best preceding term.

"Now you have the idea, I would like you to try 100."

Ensure that the pupils get the key number for 100 before trying other examples like 25, 150, 200.

The key numbers in each of the above are 62, 16, 93 and 124 respectively. The rest of the investigation explores the relationship between the key number and the given starting number.

"The starting numbers are all bigger than the key numbers. But how many times bigger?"

"Is this ratio always about the same?"

"Use this ratio to home-in on some other key numbers. Try 300 and a few other examples."

You can assist pupils by getting them to try numbers either side of what they expect to be the key number.

Possible extension

● The ratio you have found in the above activity gives an approximation (because you are using whole numbers) to a number that has something to do with the familiar Fibonacci sequence. See if you can find out what it is.

Leonardo of Pisa (1175?–1250?)

Leonardo, son of Bonaccio ('good nature'), was nicknamed Fibonacci.

He was born in Pisa. Brought up in Bougie on the north coast of Africa, his father was a merchant and Leonardo travelled throughout the Middle East and came into contact with Arabic mathematical practices. The Leaning Tower was begun during his lifetime but was not finished for nearly 200 years.

His most famous work, the *Liber Abaci*, was published in 1202. This book was influential in getting the Hindu–Arabic notation accepted in Europe. One of the many problems discussed in this book was:

Suppose that a pair of rabbits can produce a new pair every month from their second month onwards. If every new pair of rabbits does the same, how many pairs of rabbits will there be at the beginning of each month? (It is assumed that the rabbits live for ever.) The number at the end of each month will be

1 1 2 3 5 8 13 21 34 ...

In 1877 Eduard Lucas named it the Fibonacci sequence.

There are many interesting applications and extensions of work on the Fibonacci sequence – the golden ratio, the golden rectangle, the Fibonacci spiral, the distribution of florets in daisies, sunflowers and pine-cones, etc.

References

The Divine Proportion	H. Huntley
Learning with Colour: Mathematics	I. Adler
Mathematical Snapshots	H. Steinhaus
The Language of Maths	F. Land
Life of Science Library: Mathematics	D. Bergamini
Looking and Seeing 3	K. Rowland
Fibonacci Sequence	SMILE (0824)
Patterns in Nature	P. Stevens
The Penguin Dictionary of Curious and Interesting Numbers	D. Wells
History of Mathematics	H. Eves
Topics in Recreational Mathematics	J. H. Caldwell
Mathematical Enterprises for Schools	A. J. Cameron
The Fibonacci Numbers	N. N. Vorob'ev
Mathematics – A Human Endeavour	H. Jacobs
Riddles in Mathematics	E. Northrop
Making Mathematics, book 4	Paling, Banwell and Saunders

Seven points

Materials Rulers, angle measurers and perhaps tracing paper. Worksheets — at least three per pair of pupils.

Possible content and processes Exhaustive enumeration, classification of shapes, angle measurement. With the extension, this may also include prediction, generalisation and simple algebra.

Preamble This activity is probably best done by pupils working in pairs. It is a good idea for pupils to experiment on one worksheet and record on another.

Draw some seven-point patterns like this on the board.

Ask a pupil to draw a polygon on one of your patterns with corners at some (or all) of the dots.

You may need to discuss what a polygon is.

Ask pupils to draw different polygons on the other patterns on the board.

Expect/provoke some discussion as to what constitutes 'different'. This is best decided by the group.

"How many different polygons can you draw using these seven points?"

Give out the worksheets and allow pupils to draw their own polygons.

Allow sufficient time for this.

"Describe one of the shapes (without naming it) to your partner. See if they can work out which shape you mean."

Alternatively this could take the form of a guessing game where only yes/no answers are allowed.

"Try to name – beside each shape – as many of the polygons as you can."

A little help may be needed here, but it is best if points emerge from the pupils' own discussions.

Angle measurers and rulers should be available, but it is probably best to use 'by eye'.

These activities should encourage the use of 'geometrical' language.

It is then a nice idea to get two or three pairs to work together to produce 'their' master list – possibly as a poster.

Pupils could attempt some of these activities.

● "For each shape you have drawn, mark in any sides or angles which you think are the same."

● "Put the shapes you have drawn into groups."

For example, those having (a) a right-angle, (b) two sides the same, or (c) two sides parallel, etc.

It is best to allow the classification to arise naturally through discussion.

● "Which of the shapes will make tiling patterns?"

This may require the use of tracing paper.

● "Find the area of each of your shapes, using this triangle as your unit of area."

Some help may be needed to 'see' other unit triangles.

Possible extensions

● Write down the perimeter of each shape in terms of the distances *a* and *b* shown here.

● Find a relationship between the number of dots on the perimeter, the number of dots inside the polygon and its area in triangle units.

Rectangles within squares

Materials   2 cm squared paper, scissors, four or five large 6 × 6 squares, Blu-tak.

Possible content and processes   Rectangles, area, organising data.

Preamble   Make sure that your 6 × 6 squares are large enough to be seen by everyone and that the grid lines are clear.

Show the class one of your large 6 × 6 squares.

"Tell me anything you can about this."

> *You can expect to get responses referring to shape, lengths of sides, number of small squares, area, number of lines, . . .*

"I want to cut this into two different sized rectangles. I am only allowed to cut along horizontal or vertical grid lines. Decide which line I should cut along."

"What size rectangles does this give you?"

> *Allow time for pupils to visualise their solutions.*

Ask someone to describe where to cut. Cut as suggested.

Ask about the sizes of the two rectangles.

Stick the two rectangles on the board.

"Did anyone decide on a line which gives other sized rectangles?"

Cut as suggested on another large square and display as before.

"Can we get other sized rectangles?"

> *There are only two different pairs of rectangles. It is likely that some pupils will have arrived at these by using different cuts from those suggested. You may wish to discuss this.*

Show the class another large 6 × 6 square.

"Think of a way in which I could cut along lines of ths square so that I can make a set of *three* rectangles of different sizes. Where should I cut?"

Cut as suggested and display as before.

"Can we get other sized rectangles?"

It will soon be noticed that there is not an unique solution. Some examples are:

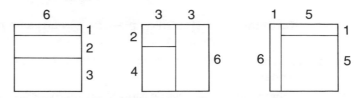

The last of these examples includes a square. Some pupils will wish to count the square as a rectangle, others not. The choice they make is not crucial, although a square **is** *in fact a rectangle, but the results will be different.*

You may wish to let pupils investigate how many different ways you can cut the 6 × 6 square into three rectangles of different sizes; this is not pursued here.

"Cut out a 6 × 6 square."

"Your task is to divide your square into as many different sized rectangles as you can."

Most pupils will cut out randomly. Others may produce a systematic approach. Some may even think of making all possible rectangles first and then try to fit the maximum number together to make the square.

Judge when to bring the class together. Ask for solutions found. Encourage descriptions of the methods used.

If squares are included, there are 8 different rectangles; if not, there are 7.

You may think it worthwhile to compare solutions and discuss their differences/similarities.

Pupils may produce more than one set of 8 (or 7) pieces. They may have different ways of putting the pieces together.

Don't be concerned if the 8 (7) solution is not found at this stage. Now may be a good time to move on.

"Working in pairs or groups, choose other sized squares to start with – it would be wise to work with squares smaller than 10 × 10."

"For each square find the maximum number of different rectangles possible."

"Keep a record of the squares which you start with and the ways in which you have divided them."

"Try to find a connection between the size of the square and the maximum number of rectangles."

As you move around the classroom, you will find opportunities to enable pupils to share their ideas on outcomes and recording.

At a later time you may draw the class together to pool ideas and discuss possible ways of organising the data and making some observations.

Discs

Materials   Cardboard or plastic discs large enough to write on and display to the class.

Possible content and processes   Whole-number arithmetic, trial and improvement, tabulation.

Preamble   The first section is an introduction to the main investigation.

"I have two discs here. I want to write a whole number on each of the four sides. Give me four different numbers."

For the first example, ask for four single-digit numbers to keep things simple. Avoidance of repetitions is not essential, but it keeps more possibilities open.

Write the numbers on the faces of the discs.

Toss the discs and ask a pupil to read the two numbers which are visible.

"What is the total of these two numbers?"

"If I toss them again will I get the same total?"

Toss the discs a few times and record the totals.

"Can I get any other totals?"

Ensure that the pupils grasp that the number of totals is limited.

Repeat the process with a new set of numbers on the discs.

You may need to repeat the process a few times before asking the questions which follow. It is important that pupils understand the process before being asked for predictions of the outcome.

"Can you tell how many totals there will be?"

"Will there always be the same number of totals?"

"Can you see how to work out the totals without tossing the discs?"

You may wish to get pupils to investigate how many totals are possible and how repeated numbers influence this. Some may discover other relationships between the numbers on the discs and the totals. Make sure that all pupils are clear about the way in which totals are generated before moving on to the main investigation.

Write 8, 10, 11, 13 on the board.

"Suppose these were the totals from tossing two discs. What numbers could have been on the discs?"

Most pupils will work by trial and improvement. You may wish to discuss systematic methods of approach if some of the preliminary work has focussed on patterns. There are several sets of starting numbers which give these totals.

Some thought will need to be given as to how to represent the numbers on the discs. Pupils come up with various suggestions. The notation must show which two numbers are on each disc; a list of four numbers is not sufficient.

Wait until several pupils have solutions. Collect them on the board and ask pupils to check that they all work.

"Are there any more solutions?"

"How can I tell if I have them all?"

Some pupils may ask about using negative numbers. It is better to use positive numbers only as this gives a finite set of solutions. Use of negative numbers could be pursued later.

"If I know one solution, can I work out the others from it?"

Look out for, and encourage, systematic approaches.

Once all the solutions have been determined, write up another set of four totals, ensuring that the sum of the largest and smallest is equal to the sum of the other two. (Why?) Ask for the solutions again.

This is normally achieved fairly quickly. If it is not, then further discussion should take place.

"If I choose *any* four totals, would I be able to find solutions? Choose some totals of your own and see if you can find solutions. If not, can you explain why?"

Pupils will approach this in a variety of ways. Others may wish to pursue some of the earlier parts of the investigations.

Possible extensions
- What happens if negative numbers are allowed?
- Repeat the investigation with three discs.
- There are three discs where it is known that the top numbers are 6, 7, 8, and that the totals are 15, 16, 17, 18, 20, 21, 22, 23. What are the bottom numbers?

Surface squares

Materials   About 50 cubes per pair or group (wooden, plastic, Multilink,...). One 3 × 3 × 3 cube made from unit cubes.

Possible content and processes   Counting, spatial skills, volume, surface area, whole-number arithmetic.

Preamble   This activity is best suited to a group of above average pupils. It is not easy to find other cuboids which have the same number of surface squares as a given shape.

Hold up the 3 × 3 × 3 cube in one hand.

"I want you to make a cube like this."

Give them time to make their own large cube.

"How many of these single cubes have you used to make the large cube?"

"Each face of the single cube is a square. How many small squares are there on one face of your large cube?"

Establish that there are 9.

"How many of these squares are there on the surface of your large cube?"

Most are likely to say 54, but some may ignore the surface touching their table and say 45. Allow time for the 54 to be agreed.

"Your 3 × 3 × 3 cube has 54 surface squares. Try to make a cuboid which also has 54 surface squares. When you find one, record it."

Some may need to discuss the meaning of cuboid.

While pupils are working on this, try to discover what strategies are being used.

There are only two more: 1 × 1 × 13 and 1 × 3 × 6.

After a while, stop the class and collect results. Encourage those who have found a solution to explain how they arrived at it.

Some may not have been successful in finding one of the two results but may have discovered a good strategy for finding the number of surface squares. It is important that pupils have the opportunity to verbalise this.

"In your pairs/groups, make a cuboid. Find the number of surface squares."

"Now make as many cuboids as you can which have this same number of surface squares. For each cuboid, keep a note of its dimensions."

You may decide to talk of surface area or square units rather than surface squares.

Check that everyone is involved in the problem.

Now prepare a table to record the results. It could look something like this:

Surface area	Size of cuboid			No. of cuboids
54	(1 × 1 × 13)	(1 × 3 × 6)	(3 × 3 × 3)	3
10		(1 × 1 × 2)		1

"When you have found a new cuboid, record its surface area and dimensions on my table. Don't forget to include the dimensions of your original cuboid."

Some may not find a second cuboid; keep an eye on this and enable them to record the details of their original cuboid.

When the table has quite a number of results, stop the activity and ask the class to look at it.

"How could we arrange these results so that we can look for patterns? Write your own 'rearranged' table."

Circulate and get pupils to talk to you about the way they are arranging the data and their reasons for doing so.

"Look at your table and write about any pattern you can find."

You may want to offer some of the following questions:

- *Is there a cuboid for an odd number of surface squares?*
- *Is there a cuboid for all even numbers of surface squares?*
- *Which cuboid gives you the largest volume for a given number of surface squares?*
- *Which cuboid gives you the smallest volume for a given number of surface squares?*
- *Can you predict possible dimensions for any given number of surface squares?*

One up, one down

Materials   Calculators (but not handed out at the start).

Possible content and processes   Estimating, pattern spotting.

Preamble   Calculators should not be used for the first part of the activity unless their use is specifically referred to in the text. At least some of the group should have done SMP 11–16 *Pencil and paper* before attempting this task.

On the board, write 30 × 40 =

"Can anyone give me the answer?"

> *Ideally, it should be arrived at mentally, although it is not essential to the activity. If no-one can do it, hand a calculator to a pupil and ask for the answer.*

Underneath 30 × 40 = 1200, write down 29 × 41 =
31 × 39 =

"What are the connections between the numbers in these calculations?"

> *Establish that in the first case you have decreased the first number (30) by one and increased the second number (40) by one. In the second, you have increased the 30 by one and decreased the 40 by one.*

"30 × 40 = 1200. Will the answer to 29 × 41 be equal to 1200, less than 1200, more than 1200? Jot down which you think will be true."

Repeat the question for 31 × 39. Ask a few pupils to give you their guesses and the reasons.

> *Allow time for discussion and argument. When you think you have pursued the issue fully . . .*

Hand a calculator to a pupil and ask for the answers to both 29 × 41 and 31 × 39. Write them on the board.

> *Discuss the answers (1189 and 1209) and their relationships to 1200. You need to establish that one is 11 less, the other is 9 more.*

On the board, write 50 × 60 =

"Can anyone give me the answer to this?"

> *Again, this should be a mental exercise. Establish the answer is 3000.*

Underneath 50 × 60 = 3000, write down 49 × 61 =
51 × 59 =

"Taking into account our previous results, jot down what you think the answers will be, or are likely to be."

Discuss their ideas and responses.

Hand a calculator to a pupil and ask for the answers to both 49 × 61 and 51 × 59. Write them on the board.

"Tell me anything you notice about these two answers."

Establish that the first answer is 11 less and second 9 more than 3000, like the results for 1200.

On the board, write 70 × 80 = 5600
                   69 × 81 =
                   71 × 79 =

"Copy these, and without doing any long multiplication or using a calculator, write down what you think the exact answers to both of these calculations will be. Compare your results with those of the person next to you."

This should not take more than a minute or two. When you have discussed the results . . .

Write on the board 50 × 90 =
                     49 × 91 =
                     51 × 89 =

"Guess what you think the answer will be in each case. Then check them out on a calculator. Discuss the results with your partner."

The fact that one answer is 41 (and not 11) less, and the other 39 (and not 9) more than 4500 often causes surprise. This needs to be discussed.

"Work in twos and threes. Try starting with some other pairs of numbers. Discuss the results you get."

It should soon be realised that the difference between the two starting numbers is the deciding factor.

Possible extensions
- What if I altered each number by 2, rather than 1?
- What if I altered each number by 3, or 4, or 7?
- What if I reduced the first number by 1 and increased the second by 2 and vice versa?
- Make up your own rules.

Frogs

Materials Pegs and pegboards or squared paper with counters of two colours, or squared paper with felt-tipped pens (two colours).

Possible content and processes Number patterns, algebra, predicting, generalising.

Preamble Before the lesson you need to place seven chairs in a row at the front of, and facing, the class.

　　Children enjoy the physical involvement at the outset; it makes the later use of materials and symbols a more personal experience. Give out materials later.

Select three boys and three girls to occupy six of the seven seats as shown below:

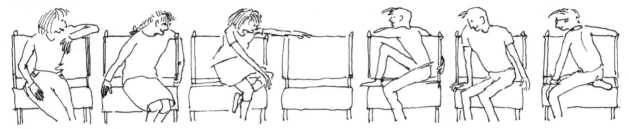

"The six people sitting in front of you are frogs! The problem they have to solve is to move so that the boy frogs change places with the girl frogs.

These frogs can only move in the following ways:

● they can slide along into an empty chair;
● they can jump over one frog into an empty chair.

　　We will watch and stop them if they break the rules."

In the early stages be prepared for movement backwards and forwards as well as noisy contributions from those watching!

When there have been several attempts at the problem you may decide to stop the action and seek ideas from the rest of the class.

"Can anyone suggest a way in which the frogs might solve their problem?"

Pupils are very ready to give verbal instructions – it clarifies the problem if you let them do this.

Continue with action and discussion until the problem has been solved.

"Did anyone notice how many moves it took?"

It is unlikely that anyone will have kept count; they are too busy solving the problem.

"The challenge is to exchange places in as few moves as possible. Let the frogs have another go at doing it – the rest of you count the number of moves. Make sure the frogs keep to the rules. Some of you could keep a note of the slides and jumps."

Recording the moves on the board using 's' and 'j' will help develop the idea of using shorthand notation; in order to distinguish between boys and girls you could use different colours.

"How many moves was that? Can it be done in fewer moves?"

There is no need to tell them that moving backwards is unnecessary unless you have 'gone wrong'; they seem to pick this up during the action!

The length of time you can usefully keep this as a class activity will depend on a number of factors – the pupils' motivation, the possibility of finding a solution quickly, your tolerance, . . .

At any time you can change the focus of action from class to pairs. Give the pupils suitable materials to try out the activity themselves – pegs and pegboards, squared paper and counters, squared paper and coloured pens.

Remind them to keep a record of their slides and jumps.

You can respond to individuals and pairs in a manner appropriate to the directions in which they seem to be going.

Find from the class their fewest number of moves. Ask one of the pupils with the least number of moves to record their moves.
For example,

sjsjjsjjjsjjsjsjs

"Can it be done in less?"

"How will you know when you have the least?"

"Is there more than one way of doing it?"

"What patterns can you see in your slides and jumps?"

"What if you had 2 girls and 2 boys (and 5 chairs); 1 girl and 1 boy (and 3 chairs); 4 girls and 4 boys (and 9 chairs); . . . 50 girls and 50 boys; . . .?

"What patterns of slides and jumps will give you the least number of moves?"

"Is there a rule connecting the number of frogs and the least number of moves?"

Possible extensions
- How does the problem change if there are two spare chairs?
- What happens if the number of girls is different from the number of boys?

Point to point

Materials — Squared paper.

Possible content and processes — Area, tabulating, predicting, checking.

Preamble — This investigation supports the work of SMP 11–16 level 2(a) *Area 1*. Pupils should know how to find the area of a rectangle.

Draw these patterns on the board.

"I have joined six tiles using certain rules. What are my rules?"

> *The rules are that tiles join at corners only and at right-angles. Accept all suggestions, but draw counter-examples to eliminate suggested rules which are not compatible with these.*
>
> *Pupils must grasp the rules before you can move on.*

"What other patterns can you make with six tiles?"

"Draw some of them."

> *Do not spend too long on this. The purpose is to clarify the rules, and show that different patterns are possible. Finding the number of different patterns for different numbers of tiles makes a separate investigation!*
>
> *Judge when to bring the class together.*

"Sometimes people like to cut out their patterns and stick them in their books. To make them look neat, they often cut out a rectangle round each pattern. So with these patterns (refer to those on the board) they would cut round them like this."

Draw round original patterns.

> *Make sure that pupils understand not to leave borders or use oblique rectangles.*

"On each of your patterns draw the rectangle round it."

> *Circulate and check that pupils are doing this correctly.*

"Find the area of each rectangle and write it down."

"What is the smallest area anyone has found so far?" Record this.

"What is the largest area anyone has found so far?" Record this.

"Can anyone find a smaller one?"

"Can anyone find a larger one?"

Give the pupils a fairly short time to convince themselves that they have found the smallest and largest areas. Do not give too much away at this stage. It is better for pupils to discover for themselves which patterns give the smallest and largest areas. More than one pattern will give the smallest area.

"Take different numbers of tiles and find the smallest and largest areas for each one. See if you can find any patterns in the numbers."

Pupils realise quite quickly that the largest area is a square, but they do not find the smallest area so easily. Drawing a table of values will help. Encourage them to predict and check their results.

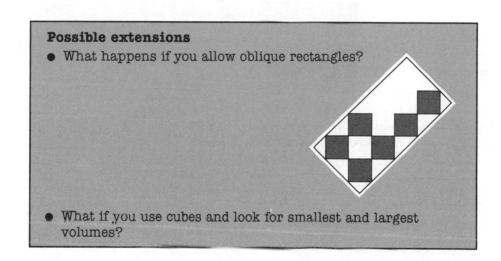

Possible extensions

● What happens if you allow oblique rectangles?

● What if you use cubes and look for smallest and largest volumes?

About about a half

Materials Worksheet, calculators, scissors, tracing paper.

Possible content and processes Comparing fractions, ideas of a limit, probably triangular and square numbers, fractions to decimals.

Preamble This activity supports SMP 11–16 level 2(b) *Fractions 3* and probably the *Fractions and decimals* booklets.

You will need to draw several squares of the same size on the board, divided into smaller squares, 3 × 3, 4 × 4, 5 × 5.

Pupils will need the worksheet of squares (3 × 3, 4 × 4, ..., 8 × 8).

On a 3 × 3 square on the board, shade squares like this.

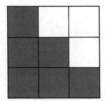

"I have shaded part of this square. How much is shaded? Is it half? . . . more than a half? . . . less than a half? What fraction has been shaded?"

> *Encourage as varied a response as possible. Some may say 6 squares, others $\frac{6}{9}$; someone may say $\frac{2}{3}$. Whatever the response, ask for reasons. Record responses but be sure to include $\frac{6}{9}$.*

On the 4 × 4 square shade squares like this.

"Here is another square – how much of this one has been shaded? Is it a half, less than a half, more than a half? What fraction has been shaded?"

> *Again encourage different responses and record them. Make sure you record $\frac{10}{16}$.*

"What can you say about the amount shaded in each large square?"

> *The same questions may lead some to say they are the same. Ask pupils to justify their responses.*

"Which is larger, $\frac{6}{9}$ or $\frac{10}{16}$?"

"Which of these is nearer a half? – Why?"

If pupils are struggling with the comparison, ask them to do the shading on the 3 × 3 and 4 × 4 squares on their worksheet. The shaded area could then be traced or cut out for comparison. Alternatively a calculator could be used to convert $\frac{6}{9}$ and $\frac{10}{16}$ to decimals. Their closeness to a half is easily observed and discussed.

"Use the worksheet. On the 5 × 5 square shade in the same way as I have done on the board."

You will need to circulate to see they have the correct shading.

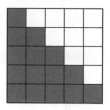

"What fraction of your square is shaded?"

"Is this larger or smaller than $\frac{6}{9}$ and $\frac{10}{16}$?"

"Which is nearest to a half?"

Presenting these fractions in a line: $\frac{6}{9}, \frac{10}{16}, \frac{15}{25}$ may suggest to some the next fraction for the 6 × 6 square.

"Now work in pairs. Using either the squares on the worksheet or by any other method, find the fractions shaded for 6 × 6, 7 × 7, 8 × 8, . . . squares. How do these compare in size with the ones we already have? Which is nearest to a half?"

For those who continue with the shading, the sequence of fractions $\frac{6}{9}$, $\frac{10}{16}, \frac{15}{25}, \frac{21}{36}, \frac{28}{49}, \frac{36}{64}$ will appear. Some may produce them by noticing the pattern of $\frac{\text{triangular numbers}}{\text{square numbers}}$.

The use of a calculator will produce a sequence of $0.666\ldots, 0.625, 0.6, 0.5833\ldots, 0.572428\ldots, 0.5625$, which will give guidance about the 'tendency' towards a half.

At some point you could draw the class together to discuss their results.

The way in which this has been developed starts the sequence with $\frac{6}{9}$ . . . Pupils could be asked if there are any fractions before this — $\frac{3}{4}$? $\frac{1}{1}$?

Possible extensions

- Some pupils could look at the algebra involved for the
  $$\frac{nth\ triangular\ number}{nth\ square\ number}$$

- If the fractions are reduced to their lowest term, what patterns can be observed in the resulting fractions?
  Note: the cancelled fractions have the Farey property
  $$\frac{p_{n-1}}{q_{n-1}} > \frac{p_n}{q_n}\ \text{because}\ p_{n-1}\,q_n = p_n q_{n-1} + 1.$$

Organising fractions

Materials	Large sheets of paper, felt-tip markers.
Possible content and processes	Fractions, classifying, tabulating, equivalence.
Preamble	This is not a teaching exercise in fractions. However, it can be useful in pinpointing strengths and weaknesses in pupils' understanding of fractions. It also focuses on the usefulness of a systematic approach.

"Give me a (counting) number less than 10. Give me another, . . . and another, . . . and another."

Record the numbers on the board.

In the following, the four numbers chosen are assumed to be 2, 8, 7, 5.

"Make me a fraction using one of these digits on top and one underneath."

"Make me some more."

Record these fractions on the board.

"Are any more allowed?"

At this stage, the aim is to make a collection of fractions, positioned randomly. Various questions may arise here or later:
"Can we use the same number twice?"
"Is $\frac{5}{2}$ allowed?"
"Isn't $\frac{2}{8}$ really $\frac{1}{4}$?"

These give an opportunity to deal with 'improper' fractions (accept these of course!), fractions equivalent to 1 (accept all of $\frac{2}{2}, \frac{5}{5}, \frac{7}{7}, \frac{8}{8}$), and equivalence of fractions like $\frac{2}{8}$ and $\frac{1}{4}$ (record as $\frac{2}{8}$).

You may decide to keep the class at this activity until they think they have exhausted the possibilities.

"Have we got them all?"

"Working in small groups, look at our fractions and see if you can organise them in some way which would help us to see if we have missed any. Fill in gaps."

Judge when to draw the class together to pool their ideas. Show each group's ideas.

These might include the following:

	2	5	7	8
2	$\frac{2}{2}$	$\frac{2}{5}$	$\frac{2}{7}$	$\frac{2}{8}$
5	$\frac{5}{2}$	$\frac{5}{5}$	$\frac{5}{7}$	$\frac{5}{8}$
7	$\frac{7}{2}$	$\frac{7}{5}$	$\frac{7}{7}$	$\frac{7}{8}$
8	$\frac{8}{2}$	$\frac{8}{5}$	$\frac{8}{7}$	$\frac{8}{8}$

or

②	$\frac{2}{2}$	$\frac{5}{2}$	$\frac{7}{2}$	$\frac{8}{2}$
⑤	$\frac{2}{5}$	$\frac{5}{5}$	. . .	
⑦	. . .			
⑧	. . .			

or

$\frac{8}{2}$ $\frac{7}{2}$ $\frac{5}{5}$ $\frac{8}{5}$ . . .

in order

"Did anyone find any new fractions?"

"Have we found them all?"

Continue the discussion until pupils are convinced that they have found all the fractions. This stage may include adding fractions to some displays.

Take each table or list in turn. Ask for comments and encourage discussion about each.

The focus of the activity now changes to spotting patterns and relationships within each display. These might include:
- *increasing/decreasing fractions in a row or column,*
- *fractions greater than/less than 1,*
- *fractions equivalent to 1,*
- *number of different fractions,*
- *equivalence, etc.*

"In your group, decide on the method of display you like best. Choose another set of four numbers and make all the fractions you can. Write comments on your results; number of fractions, number of different fractions, patterns, . . . Organise the results from your group on a large sheet of paper so that the rest of the class can look at them."

During this period you may find examples of four numbers where:
- *numbers are factors of others (1, 2, 3, 6).*
- *a number has been used more than once (2, 2, 5, 7).*

This will cause the maximum number of different fractions to vary and present a further line of enquiry.

Collect some examples of individual displays and comments to show the possible variations.

Possible extensions
- How does the number of different fractions depend on the four numbers chosen?

Moving shapes

Materials   Card, scissors, pairs of compasses, rulers.

Possible content and processes   Loci, constructions, spatial awareness, patterns, possibly measurement of straight and curved lines, perimeter, area, circumference.

Preamble   This is a very open-ended investigation and pupils should be encouraged to follow and develop their own particular lines of interest. At times they will be asked to work individually, but at other times it is advisable to suggest they work in pairs.

     During the time pupils are imagining the shapes, be sure to give them plenty of time to manipulate their images – dots between instructions indicate where time should be given.

"Close your eyes . . . In your mind, picture a square . . . Hold it still . . . Try to keep it in the centre of your picture . . . Make your square bigger . . . make it smaller . . . make it any size you like . . . Hold that square in your mind . . . A circle now appears on top of your square, resting on its top edge . . . Hold that picture of your square and circle . . . The circle now begins to roll along the top edge . . . Then it rolls down the side . . . along the bottom edge . . . up the last edge until it returns to its starting point."

"Concentrate on your circle for a few seconds. A little hole appears at the centre of the circle, just large enough to put a pencil point through. Roll the circle around the square once more . . . slowly . . . leaving a pencil trail as it goes . . . along the top edge . . . down the side . . . along the bottom edge . . . up the last edge until it reaches its starting point."

"Open your eyes when you are ready. On your paper, draw the path your pencil made as it moved with the circle around the square."

Allow pupils enough time to record their images.

"Compare your drawing with that of your partner. Discuss any differences."

"Each pair now join up with another pair and compare and discuss your drawings."

At the appropriate time, ask a few pupils to describe to the class what they think the path looks like.

The main argument is usually about what happens at the corners. Some will argue that it is a curved path, others that it is a sloping path, others will think it is a right-angle.

After listening to pupils' ideas, invite them to test their ideas out for themselves.

When you have established what really happens at the corners . . .

"So far, we have had a circle rolling around a square. But what if I had chosen to roll a circle around an equilateral triangle, or around a parallelogram?"

"What if I had chosen to roll a square around a triangle or around another square? What trail would the centre take then? There are lots of combinations you can try. Choose one and see what you can find out. Remember, we want to know what trail the centre of the rolling shape makes as it travels around the stationary one. Try to see it in your mind first and draw what you think the trail will be."

Give pupils the freedom to experiment and record as they wish.

Give them opportunities to share their ideas, recording, results and findings with the whole class.

Finding the centre of, say, an isosceles triangle causes much argument, but this is only to be encouraged.

Possible extensions
- What if we look at a point on the perimeter of the shape, rather than the centre? What path does this point trace out?
- What trail does the corner of a square trace out as it rolls, say, around another square?
- Is there a relationship between the length of the path the point takes and the perimeter of the moving shape? Or the perimeter of the stationary shape? Or both?
- What if we roll a shape along a straight line? What path does its centre make, and what path does a point on its perimeter make? How long is one cycle of this path? Does the length of this cycle have anything to do with the perimeter of the rolling shape?
- Given the drawings, is it possible to tell which shapes have been used?

Geometric Images (ATM) gives some useful related ideas.

Filling boxes

Materials   Cubes (Multilink or centicubes) available, but not handed out initially. Several ready-made 4 × 4 × 4 blocks and a 4 × 4 × 4 box without a lid into which a block *just* fits.

Possible content and processes   Spatial awareness, number patterns, generalising.

Preamble   Pupils should have sufficient recent experience of working with cubes to be able to handle the first three introductory questions. There are links with SMP 11–16 *Squaring and cubing*, 3(b) *Squares and cubes* and 2(b) *Three dimensions 2*.

"I have here some small cubes and a box without a lid."

"How many of these small cubes do you think will fit along each edge of my box?"

Make pupils use their eyes first. Only then let someone check.

"Each edge of my box is as long as four small cubes. What shape is the box?"

"Draw a picture of my box."

Those who manage a reasonable sketch will have something to use later when tackling questions about the box. Those who don't, may need early access to a made-up 4 × 4 × 4 cube.

"I want to fill this box completely with small cubes. How many small cubes will I need?"

Encourage any pupils who get stuck at this stage to think how many small cubes would be needed to cover the bottom of your box. Make sure pupils can visualise the 64 small cubes in four 4 × 4 layers – both horizontally and vertically. (Use your/their ready-made blocks.)

Place your ready-made 4 × 4 × 4 block inside your open-topped box.

"Now work in pairs to decide how many small cubes are touching the sides and the bottom of my box."

Place the box, with its contents, in a position where all pupils can see it (preferably raised and tilted, so that the top is visible).

This initial task is deliberately specific. It requires pupils to count intelligently – avoiding double counting of small cubes which touch more than one face of the box. The purpose is not merely 'to get the answer'. If a pair asks "Is it 80?" or "Is it 52?", don't answer "Yes" or "No" but ask them to explain how they got their answer. If necessary, help them to reconsider ("Could it really be as many as 80? How many small cubes are there altogether?").

Working without apparatus can help pupils to structure their counting intelligently, so don't be too quick to resort to concrete materials. However, some pairs will need to handle a 4 × 4 × 4 arrangement of small cubes sooner rather than later.

*When a pair is ready, invite them to tackle the general problem below –
better presented orally to each pair. Choose a good moment to bring
the class together to review the 4 × 4 × 4 case.*

"Suppose we fill open-topped boxes of different sizes with small cubes.
Can you find a general rule which will tell you how many small cubes
touch the sides and the bottom of the box?"

*Pupils should start with boxes which are different sized cubes. Pupils
will find it helpful to look at boxes both smaller and bigger than the
4 × 4 × 4. Pupils should draw up some kind of table:*

Side length	1	2	3	4	5	6	100
Number touching sides or bottom	1	8	25	52	?	?	?

+7 +17 +?

*Their table may suggest a likely answer for 5 × 5 × 5, then 6 × 6 × 6
boxes, and so on. Some pupils may be able to extend this to predict
what happens for a box of side 100.*

*Very few pupils will notice the (often useful) idea of counting cubes
which do touch the sides or bottom of the box, simply by subtracting
those which do not touch from the total number. Do not foist this
beautiful idea on pupils too soon. It is best saved until you review the
problem with the whole class after marking their write-ups.*

*Encourage pupils to structure their counting in a way which will allow
them to deal with larger cubes efficiently. For example:*

3 × 3 × 3
(bottom = 3 × 3) + (sides = 4 × (2 × 2), or 4 × (3 × 2) − 4 × 2)

4 × 4 × 4
(bottom = 4 × 4) + (sides = 4 × (3 × 3), or 4 × (4 × 4) − 4 × 3)
so **5 × 5 × 5**
⋮
so **n × n × n**

Possible extensions
- What happens if the box has a lid?
- What happens if the box is a cuboid?

Tower of Hanoi

Materials   Tower of Hanoi – for demonstration purposes. Worksheet – preferably duplicated on card. Micro with 'Hanoi' program – if available. Scissors.

Possible content and processes   Strategy, tabulating, recognising patterns, predicting, verifying, powers of 2, large numbers.

Preamble   A well-known investigation giving scope to a wide ability range.

"In a distant land there is a temple, and in the temple there are three golden rods. The priests say that when the universe was created, 64 golden discs were placed on one of the end rods, with the largest disc at the bottom and decreasing in size to the top.

Every day, a priest moves one disc from one rod to another. He can only move each disc onto a larger disc or an empty rod.

The priests say that when all the discs are piled in order of size on the rod at the other end, the universe will come to an end."

Make this introduction interesting and 'alive', embellishing it as necessary. Pupils like being put in an imaginary situation.

"So that you can get the idea, I'm going to start with a tower of only three discs. How many moves would this take to transfer all the discs?"

Take a few suggestions before moving on.

Get a pupil to move the discs. Ask the rest of the class to check that the rules are obeyed, and to count the moves.

Make sure that all pupils understand the rules – in particular that a larger disc cannot go on a smaller one.

"What is the smallest number of moves?"

Continue this until there is general agreement on the smallest number (7).

"Now I want you to practise with three and four discs. Work in pairs. Check that you can transfer three discs in seven moves. Look for the smallest number of moves for four discs. Keep a note of your moves."

Hand out the worksheet and explain how it can be used. The squares are to be cut out to represent the discs.

Find the smallest number achieved for four discs and get someone to demonstrate how they did it.

"Now that you have the idea, let's go back to 64 discs. If the universe were created today, how long do you think it would last? Remember that one disc is moved each day."

Write their guesses on the board.

"How can we check these answers?"

"Now try with 5, 6, 7, . . . discs and record your results. Are there any other simple values you can find? (1 and 2 discs.) See if all these values can help you predict the number of moves for 64 discs. Work in pairs, one of you making the moves and the other checking on the rules and counting."

"What patterns have you found?"
"Can you now make a prediction for 64 discs?"

"What happens when you work this out on a calculator?"

Discuss such things as:

- *the largest number a calculator can store,*
- *how to deal with larger numbers (work in millions or billions),*
- *scientific notation,*
- *approximation.*

From the number of moves, an estimate of the life of the imaginary universe can be made, in days or years.

The number of moves can be calculated from $2^{64} - 1$. This is 18446744073709551615. This is roughly 50000000000000000 years at the rate of one move per day! Even if the priests moved the discs at one per second, and made no mistakes, they would still take nearly 600000000000 years!

An historical note

The Tower of Hanoi problem was first posed in 1883 by Eduard Lucas. The fictitious story of the priests was only added a year later. Here is the original version:

In the great temple at Benares, beneath the dome which marks the centre of the world, rests a brass plate in which are fixed three diamond needles, each a cubit high and as thick as the body of a bee. On one of these needles, at the creation, God placed 64 discs of pure gold, the largest disc resting on the brass plate, and the others getting smaller and smaller up to the top one. This is the Tower of Bramah. Day and night unceasingly the priests transfer the discs from one diamond needle to another according to the fixed and immutable laws of Bramah, which require that the priest on duty must not move more than one disc at a time and that he must place this disc on a needle so that there is no smaller disc below it. When the 64 discs have been thus transferred from the needle on which at the creation God placed them to one of the other needles, tower, temple and Brahmins alike will crumble into dust, and with a thunderclap the world will vanish.

Worksheets

Arithmogons

Name ....

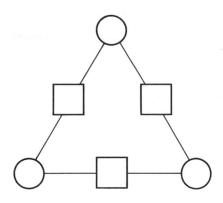
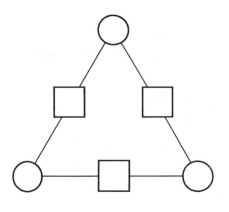

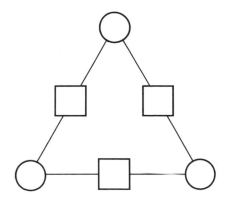
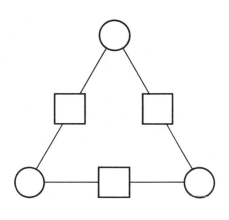

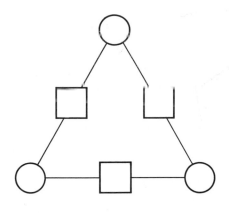
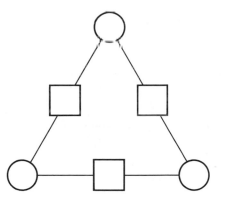

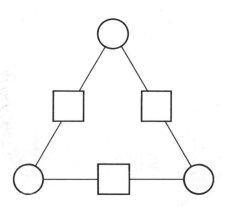
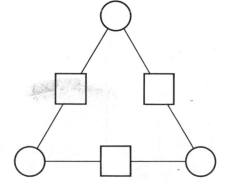

Number and patterns 1

Name ....

1										
1	1									
1	2	1								
1	3	3	1							
1	4	6	4	1						
1	5	10	10	5	1					
1						1				
1							1			
1								1		
1									1	
1										1
1										
1										

Number and patterns 2

1							
1	2						
1	3						

Seven points

Name ....

About about a half Name ....

Tower of Hanoi

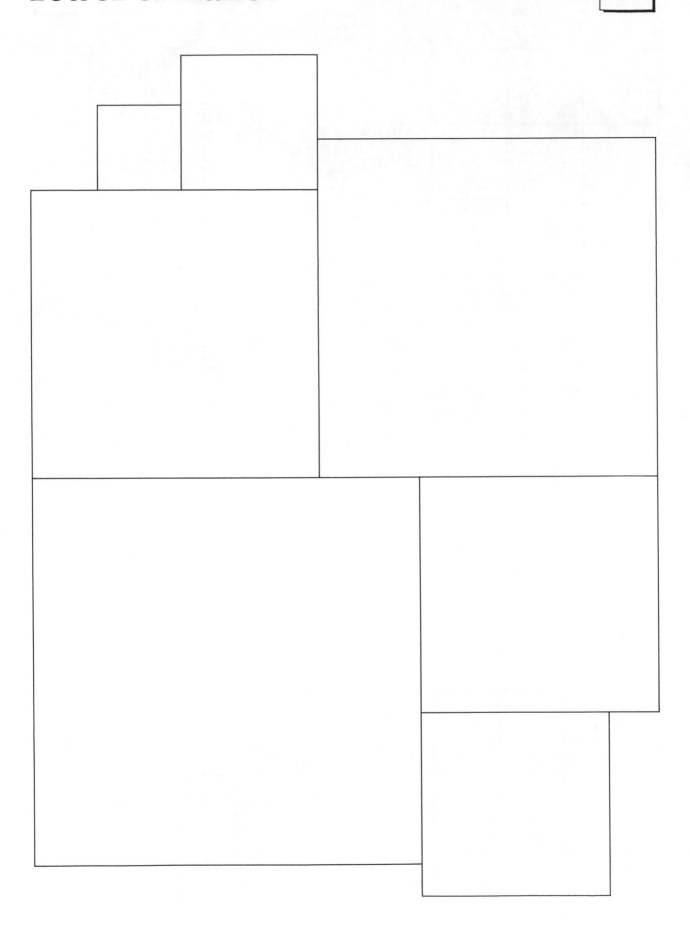

Square spotty paper

Triangular spotty paper